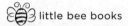 little bee books

A division of Bonnier Publishing
853 Broadway, New York, New York 10003
Copyright © 2016 by Bonnier Publishing
All rights reserved, including the right of reproduction in whole or in part in any form.
LITTLE BEE BOOKS is a trademark of Bonnier Publishing Group, and associated colophon is a trademark of Bonnier Publishing Group.
Manufactured in the United States   LB 0216
First Edition 10 9 8 7 6 5 4 3 2 1

Library of Congress Cataloging-in-Publication Data:
Names: Ohlin, Nancy, author. | Larkum, Adam, illustrator.
Title: Blast Back! : Ancient Greece / by Nancy Ohlin ; illustrated by Adam Larkum.
Other titles: Ancient Greece
Description: New York, N.Y.: little bee books, an imprint of Bonnier Publishing Group, [2016] | Includes bibliographical references. | Audience: Grades 4 to 6.
Subjects: LCSH: Greece—History—To 146 B.C.—Juvenile literature. | Greece—Civilization—To 146 B.C.—Juvenile literature.
Classification: LCC DF215 .O45 2016 | DDC 938—dc23
LC record available at http://lccn.loc.gov/2015039048

Identifiers: LCCN 2015039048
ISBN 9781499801187 (pbk); ISBN 9781499801194 (hc); ISBN 9781499804027 (eBook)

littlebeebooks.com
bonnierpublishing.com

ANCIENT GREECE

by Nancy Ohlin   illustrated by Adam Larkum

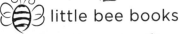
little bee books

CONTENTS

EUROPE

MEDITERRANEAN SEA

ANCIENT GREECE

AFRICA

Introduction

When you hear people talk about ancient Greece, you might think of things like Greek mythology and the Parthenon. But what was ancient Greece *really* like? Was it ruled by kings and queens? What did kids do for fun? And what was the Parthenon for, anyway?

Let's blast back in time for a little adventure and find out. . . .

A Brief History of Ancient Greece

You're wondering: What exactly is ancient Greece?

Ancient Greece was a civilization. "Civilization" means the society, culture, and way of life of a particular time and place. It's "ancient" because it's thousands of years old. "Greece" refers to the country in Europe. However, there was no actual country called "Greece" back then. Greece was more like a collection of communities that governed themselves.

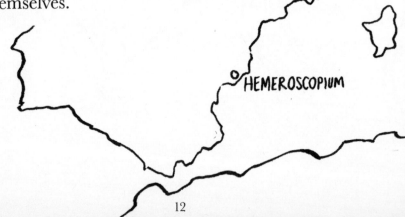

HEMEROSCOPIUM

TANAIS

CHERSONESUS

TRAPEZUS

SINOPE

BYZANTIUM

PELLA

NEAPOLIS

TARENTUM

PHOCAEA

TARSUS

CROTON

ATHENS

SPARTI

TYRE

SYRACUSE

CARTHAGE

NAUCRATIS

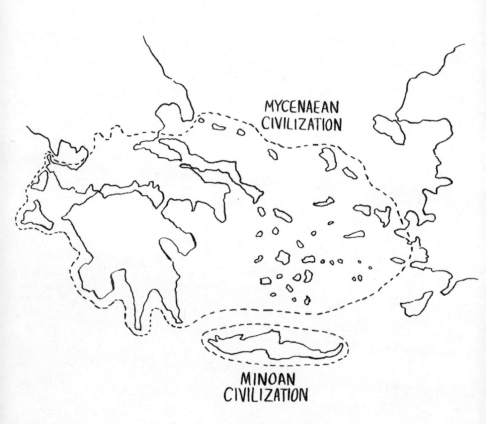

So just who were the ancient Greeks? What made a person from that time "Greek"?

From around 3000 BCE to nearly 1000 BCE, two important civilizations existed in the Mediterranean region: the Minoan civilization and the Mycenaean civilization. The Minoans, who came first, were based in the city of Knossos on the island of Crete. The Mycenaeans, who eventually conquered the Minoans, were based in the city of Peloponnesus on the Greek peninsula.

Around 1150 BCE, the Mycenaean civilization came to an end. This started a period called the "Dark Age." It was the Dark Age because things were pretty chaotic and gloomy; also, historians don't know a whole lot about this time.

MYCENAEAN

1150 BCE

END OF THE MYCENAEAN AGE

During the Dark Age and beyond, groups of Mycenaeans migrated all over the Greek peninsula and also to other places around the Mediterranean Sea. They set up trading posts. Some mingled with and married people from other cultures. Small communities began to form in these spots.

These widespread communities had much in common. They spoke Greek, shared the same religion, and had similar customs. Still, these communities were very independent and distinct.

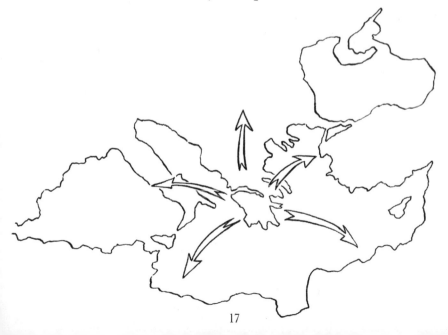

These communities gradually morphed into actual cities. But the cities still didn't come together under one government; there was no united "Greece" in ancient Greece.

The ancient Greek civilization lasted for several more centuries after the formation of the cities. It came to an end after being conquered by the Macedonians and the Romans.

Now, more than two thousand years later, we consider ancient Greece to be one of the most important and influential civilizations in history.

The Cradle of Western Civilization

Ancient Greece is sometimes referred to as the "cradle of Western civilization" because it helped to nurture many important civilizations (and cultures and ideas) that came after it, much like a cradle helps to nurture a baby.

Geography and Climate

Today, Greece is a country in the southern part of Europe. It is bordered by three seas: the Mediterranean Sea to the south, the Ionian Sea to the west, and the Aegean Sea to the east. To the north and northeast, it is bordered by the countries of Albania, Bulgaria, the Republic of Macedonia, and Turkey. Greece has more than two thousand islands.

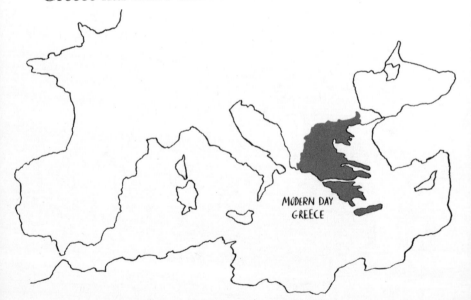

MODERN DAY
GREECE

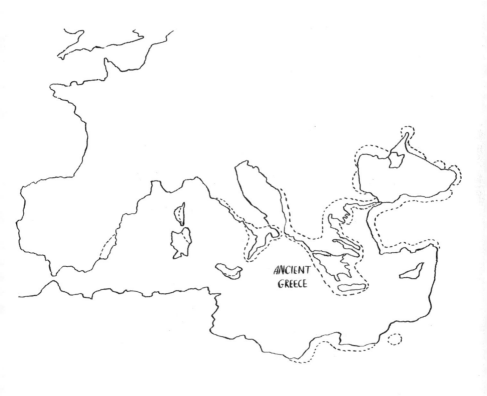

The borders of ancient Greece are less clear. They shifted around due to migrations and wars. But generally speaking, the ancient Greek settlements included the Greek mainland, the islands of Crete and Sicily, southern Italy, and part of Turkey.

Greece has always been mountainous and rocky—and also hot and dry, with little rain. This made farming difficult, and people fought over the most fertile plots of land. The best crops for the Greek climate included olives, which could be made into olive oil; grapes, which could be made into wine; and barley. The ancient Greeks traded these and other goods among themselves as well as with people in other lands, like Egypt.

Because ancient Greece was so mountainous, the best way to get around was by boat. People also traveled by donkey, since donkeys could go up and down hills.

City-States

What is a "city-state"? And how could a place be both a city and a state? (A city is a large town, and a state is a territory that governs itself.)

Remember those small separate communities that sprouted up all over Greece and elsewhere during and after the Dark Age?

Over time, these communities grew into poleis, or city-states. A city-state is a city surrounded by countryside; it also rules itself, like a state. City-states in ancient Greece would sometimes go to war against one another. Or they might join forces to fight other city-states or common enemies.

These city-states were a natural outcome of the geography of Greece. All the mountains made travel and communication difficult. This meant that the communities were naturally isolated and forced to take care of themselves.

A city-state was usually built around a central plot of high ground, like a hill or a large rock; this high ground was referred to as an "acropolis" or "citadel." Important buildings usually sat on top of it. If invaders showed up, it was easier to defend from above.

There were hundreds of city-states in ancient Greece. The most famous and important one was Athens. At its peak, Athens produced artists, writers, thinkers, and other great minds whose ideas shaped and continue to shape today's Western world.

Another famous and important city-state was Sparta, which was known for its amazing military. All Spartan males had to serve in the army. Spartan boys were taken away from their families at age seven to begin their military training.

Athens still exists as a modern city. Sparta is no more, although a new city, Sparti, sits on a portion of the old Sparta site.

City-States Outside of Greece

Ancient Greece wasn't the first or only civilization to have city-states. There were city-states as far back as 5000 BCE in Mesopotamia, in the area now known as Iraq. There were many city-states in Europe in the Middle Ages, including Venice, Florence, and Geneva. Modern-day Singapore is a city-state.

The Birth of Democracy

Several forms of government existed in ancient Greece, including monarchy, oligarchy, and tyranny. In a monarchy, a king or queen is the ruler. (Queens rarely ruled in ancient Greece, however.) Oligarchy is rule by a few, like a small group of wealthy men. (An aristocracy is a type of oligarchy.) Tyranny means that one person has seized power without the right to do so. (A dictator is a kind of tyrant.)

The city-state of Athens, under the leadership of a man named Pericles, came up with another form of government: democracy, or rule by the people. Under Athenian democracy, citizens had lots of rights. They could vote. They could become government officials. They could serve on juries to decide if accused criminals were guilty or innocent. They could attend a public gathering called the "Assembly" with thousands of other Athenians to discuss important matters of law and policy.

But "rule by the people" didn't mean all people. To be considered a citizen of Athens, you had to be a man over the age of twenty. If you were a woman, a child, a foreigner, or a slave, you didn't get to participate in the democratic process.

Today, many countries including Greece have a democratic form of government or some elements of democracy.

Slaves

Historians estimate that anywhere from two-fifths to four-fifths of all Athenians were slaves. Being a slave meant that you were owned by another person and were forced to perform labor. Slaves worked in a variety of settings—anywhere from private homes and farms to factories and mines.

When Athenians conquered a city-state or other territory, they might turn its residents into slaves. They were also not above kidnapping outsiders and turning them into slaves.

Ancient Greek slaves did have some opportunities to become free. They were paid, which meant that they could save enough money to buy their freedom. A generous or grateful master might decide to let his slave go. Still, a freed slave could never become a real citizen.

Slaves also existed elsewhere and at other times in ancient Greece. But Athens stands out because slavery was such an important part of its society. Sadly, one of the reasons that Athenians accomplished so much was because they had slaves to do their menial labor for them.

The Slave Who Helped Save Athens

Sicinnus was a slave who belonged to the Greek leader and general Themistocles. During an invasion of Greece, Sicinnus helped his master win the Battle of Salamis by feeding a false story to the enemy's commander, Xerxes.

Gods and Goddesses

The ancient Greeks believed that deities were all-powerful and determined every aspect of their lives. If you got sick, it was probably because you had displeased an immortal being. The same applied to bad weather, a poor harvest, or defeat in battle.

Accordingly, the ancient Greeks prayed to their gods and goddesses a lot. Religious festivals, ceremonies, and sacrifices were an essential part of society. The Greeks also sought divine advice through magical devices called oracles that allowed them to have "conversations" with deities.

Each god or goddess had a purpose or function, starting with the creation of the world. We know this from Greek myths, which are stories based on religious beliefs.

According to one creation myth, the earth goddess, Gaea, emerged from chaos and gave birth to the sky god, Uranus. Gaea and Uranus had many children; twelve of them, along with some of their children, were called the "Titans." The Titans were the first rulers of the world.

After them came Zeus, who was the king of the next generation of gods and goddesses. Zeus was the son of two Titans named Cronus and Rhea but was not a Titan himself.

Zeus was one of the Olympians, who were the ancient Greeks' most important deities. They were called the "Olympians" because they were said to live on Mount Olympus (which is a real mountain

in Greece that still exists today). Besides Zeus, the other Olympians were: Hera, Aphrodite, Apollo, Ares, Artemis, Athena, Demeter, Hephaestus, Hermes, Hestia, Poseidon, and Dionysus.

There were many other gods and goddesses as well, and also demigods and demigoddesses. ("Demi" meant that they were half deities or simply minor deities.)

The Olympians

Each of the Olympians had special roles and powers. For example:

Aphrodite was the goddess of love, fertility, and beauty. Her son Eros (aka Cupid) did her bidding by shooting arrows into people's hearts to make them fall in love.

Apollo was the god and protector of many things, including music, poetry, health, youth, beauty, and prophecy.

Athena was the goddess of war and wisdom, and a protector of cities, especially Athens.

Poseidon was the god of the sea, earthquakes, and horses.

Pandora's Box

The expression "Pandora's box" refers to something that causes unexpected problems. It comes from the Greek myth of Pandora, who gave her husband, Epimetheus, a box (or possibly a jar). When Epimetheus opened it, all the evils of the world were released. (The box was a "present" from Zeus, who wanted to punish Epimetheus and his brother Prometheus for various crimes.)

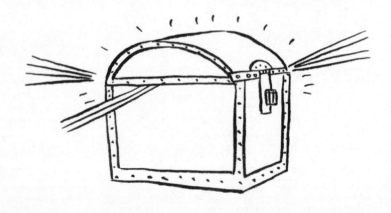

Temples and Other Architecture

The ancient Greeks were famous for their architecture. "Architecture" means the designing and constructing of buildings and other structures.

The Greeks were especially famous for all the temples they built in honor of their gods and goddesses. The purpose of the temples was to house statues of these sacred beings. Many of these temples still stand in Greece today. The most famous of them is the Parthenon, which was built for Athena on top of a well-known acropolis (or high ground) in Athens called the "Acropolis." The Parthenon was designed by two famous architects named Ictinus and Callicrates.

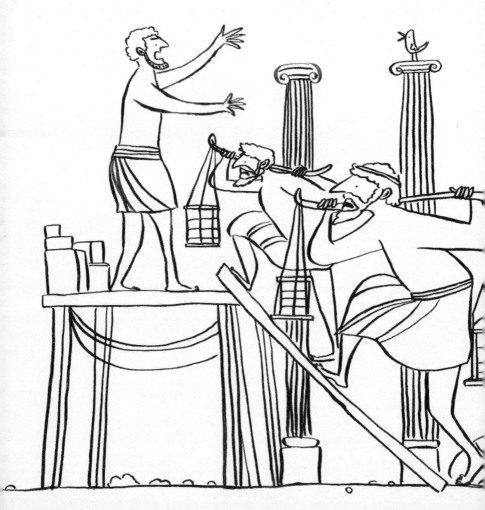

The ancient Greeks also built other types of buildings, like city and government buildings, theaters, and stadiums. A building team typically consisted of one or more head architects; workers to dig up and transport marble and limestone from quarries; carvers to carve these materials into blocks; laborers to hoist these blocks into place; metalworkers; painters; sculptors; and others.

There were three major orders, or styles, in Greek architecture: Doric, Ionic, and Corinthian. The Doric order used columns and capitals. A capital is an element that sits on top of the column. With the Doric order, the capital might be a square block or other simple shape. With the Ionic order, the capitals tended to look like spiral scrolls. With the Corinthian order, the capitals were carved with a fancy design that resembled the leaves of the acanthus plant.

The Seven Wonders of the Ancient World

The ancient Greeks built (or contributed to the building of) five of the seven wonders:

The Temple of Artemis at Ephesus

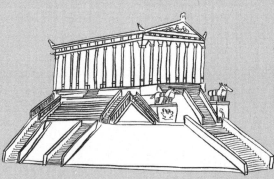

The Statue of Zeus at Olympia

The Colossus of Rhodes (a statue)

The Mausoleum at Halicarnassus (a tomb)

The Pharos of Alexandria (a lighthouse)

The two other wonders are the Hanging Gardens of Babylon and the Pyramids of Giza. Of the original seven wonders, only the Pyramids of Giza still remain.

The Olympics

You've probably watched the Olympic Games on TV or maybe even seen them in person. Did you know that this athletic festival dates all the way back to at least 776 BCE? That's almost three thousand years ago!

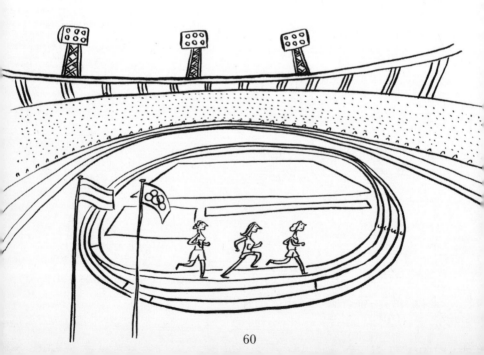

The first Olympic Games took place on the ancient Greek site of Olympia. According to myth, the festival was founded by Heracles, the half-mortal son of Zeus, in honor of Zeus. The games were held every four years; that four-year stretch is a measure of time called an "Olympiad."

In the beginning, the only event at the Olympics was a short footrace called a "stade." (The word "stadium" comes from stade.) Eventually, more events were added, including wrestling, throwing the discus and javelin, boxing, and chariot racing. At first, women were not allowed to compete, although there was a separate athletic festival for them called the "Heraea."

The Olympic Games were so important to the ancient Greeks that they would call a temporary truce to wars so the games could take place as scheduled.

The Romans put an end to the Olympic Games in 393 CE. The games were revived in 1896 through the efforts of a French educator and sportsman named Baron Pierre de Coubertin, who felt that the games would help bring countries together. They are still held every four years, although the location changes each time, and both men and women from all over the world are allowed to compete.

Famous Ancient Olympians

Milo of Croton: Milo, who lived in Greece during the sixth century BCE, won the wrestling championship in six Olympic Games and seven Pythian Games, which were similar to the Olympics. Legend has it that Milo trained by carrying an ox in his arms every day.

Melankomas of Caria: A boxer during the first century CE, he was undefeated even though he never managed to land a blow.

Everyday Life

Let's pretend that you are a child in ancient Athens. Your father is a craftsman—the ancient Greeks were famous for their crafts—and your mother takes care of the house and family.

Your father's craft is ironwork. In his workshop, he melts down iron in a hot furnace and hammers the molten metal into weapons and farming tools. Several slaves assist him. He is one of the finest craftsmen in Athens, and people come from all over to buy his wares.

Like most women, your mother is expected to stay home and take care of the house and the family. She has several female slaves to help her with the housework. She is not allowed to inherit property or even have much money.

The boys in your family go to school once they are seven. In addition to the basics like reading and writing, they learn how to memorize and recite poetry, discuss and debate ideas, and play a musical instrument or two. They also train in sports and become physically fit so that they might compete in the Olympics or serve in the military someday.

The girls in your family don't go to school. (Girls from wealthy families might learn reading and writing from private tutors, though.) Girls are supposed to know how to spin, weave, raise children, and maintain a home—skills that their mothers pass down to them. When the girls in your family become teenagers, your father will choose husbands for them.

Your house is made of unbaked mud bricks that were dried in the sun, and it has a tile roof. There are very few windows. There is an open courtyard in the middle where the women and girls do their spinning, weaving, cooking, and other tasks.

At night, your father brings his male friends home for a meal. They eat lying down on couches. A typical dinner menu might be some combination of vegetable broth, bread, olive oil, olives, cheese, fruit, honey cakes, and wine. Fish is for special occasions. While the men have their party, your mother might relax in the family room with you and the other children in your house.

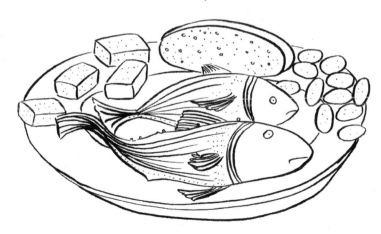

Like other Athenian men, your father spends most of his time outside your house. Much of the public life in Athens takes place in the agora, which is the marketplace. But the agora isn't just an open-air shopping mall. It's where men gather to discuss

important ideas and talk about business. Athenian men also attend plays, musical performances, and religious festivals. The women and girls do not go out in public much.

Your father might also be involved in political life—maybe as an Assembly member or jury member—or serve in the military. Women are excluded from political life, and they are not allowed to vote, either.

For clothing, both men and women wear a draped garment called a "chiton," although a man's is usually shorter than a woman's. Women wear a piece of cloth called a "peplos" over the chiton; the peplos is fastened at their shoulders. Men wear a cloak over theirs—either a short one called a "chlamys" or a long one called a "himation."

Fun and Games

For entertainment, the ancient Greeks liked to sing and play instruments such as the harp and the lyre.

The Greeks also enjoyed board games similar to backgammon, chess, and snakes and ladders. Other games included knucklebones, which was like jacks, and kottabos, which involved flicking wine at a target. Women and children also liked spinning tops.

Health, Medicine, and Science

If you got sick in ancient Greece, you believed that the gods and goddesses were responsible. Therefore, you prayed and made sacrifices to cure illness and prevent it, too.

But the ancient Greeks also developed medical treatments based on real scientific research. An ancient Greek doctor named Hippocrates is often referred to as the "father of medicine." He wrote a great deal about how the body worked. He believed that diseases had natural and not supernatural causes.

The ancient Greeks also made big strides in other areas of science, including biology, astronomy, geography, and mathematics. Ancient Greek scientists observed the world around them—including the behavior of animals, plants, human beings, and the stars—and wrote down their observations and ideas, much like scientists do today.

The Hippocratic Oath

The Hippocratic oath is a short speech that spells out the duties and responsibilities of doctors. It is believed to have been written by Hippocrates. Students today still recite it when they graduate from medical school.

Archimedes and Ptolemy

Archimedes was a brilliant scientist, mathematician, and inventor who lived from 287 to 212 BCE. He helped develop geometry, discovered the power of the lever, and figured out the principles of displacement and buoyancy. Legend has it that he created a big solar mirror to set fire to enemy ships that attacked Greece.

Ptolemy was an astronomer, mathematician, and geographer of Greek descent from the second century CE. He believed that the earth was the center of the universe.

83

Poetry and Drama

The ancient Greeks were masters of the written and spoken word.

They invented drama and were the first to have theaters. Writers wrote plays for religious festivals and competed against one another for prizes. Plays were either tragedies, in which something bad would happen to the hero, or comedies, which concerned the mishaps of lesser individuals who were not heroes. The actors always wore masks as part of their stage costumes. Famous playwrights include Aeschylus, Sophocles, Euripides, and Aristophanes.

Poetry was another important literary form. The ancient Greeks composed epic poems, which told stories about heroes, or lyric poems, which expressed thoughts and emotions. All poems were intended to be spoken out loud or sung. The ancient Greek poet Homer wrote the *Iliad*, which tells the tale of the Trojan War, and the *Odyssey*, which describes of the adventures of the legendary King Odysseus. Both poems are still read and studied today.

The Masters of Tragedy

Aeschylus, Sophocles, and Euripides were the masters of tragic drama. Some of their plays—like the *Oresteia* trilogy by Aeschylus, *Oedipus Rex* by Sophocles, and *Medea* by Euripides—are still produced today.

Philosophy

Do you ever ask yourself the "big questions"? Like: Why are we here? How does time work? Is it ever okay to lie? Is my mind the same thing as my brain?

These are philosophical questions. The word "philosophy" comes from the Greek term *philosophia*, which means love of wisdom. Philosophers are people who study and practice philosophy.

They ponder these and other big questions and try to come up with answers.

Ancient Greece was the birthplace of Western philosophy. Some of the most important philosophers in history were ancient Greeks. Many of them taught in schools. They gathered in the agoras and other public places to talk philosophy with one another and with regular citizens.

Famous Greek Philosophers

Socrates: In the fifth century BCE, Socrates wandered the streets of Athens seeking the truth and encouraging others to do the same. His approach, called the "Socratic method," was to talk to people in a back-and-forth, question-and-answer way. Socrates never wrote down any of his thoughts or teachings. We only know of them because other people recorded them and passed them on, in particular the philosopher Plato.

Plato: Plato is one of the most influential figures in the history of Western philosophy. He published several dozen books on philosophy, many of them in the form of dialogues between two or more speakers. In his early dialogues, Socrates was the main speaker. The dialogues dealt with a number of subjects, including life, love, friendship, knowledge, religion, and government. Plato also founded the Academy, an Athenian school devoted to the teaching of philosophy, law, and math, among other subjects.

Aristotle: Aristotle was one of Plato's pupils at the Academy. After Plato's death, Aristotle went on to found his own school, the Lyceum. His work went beyond Plato's teachings and extended into new philosophical ideas as well as the natural sciences (how things in nature behave) and social sciences (how human beings behave).

The End of Socrates

Some Athenians did not appreciate Socrates's ideas or methods. Several of his political enemies falsely charged him with "neglect of the gods" and "corruption of the young," and he was sentenced to death by drinking a poison called "hemlock."

The End of a Civilization

In 499 BCE, the Persians attempted to take over Greece. In response, the scattered and separate city-states joined forces to defend themselves against their common enemy. After a long series of wars, the Greeks defeated the Persians in 479 BCE.

This Greek unity did not last long. In 431 BCE, the two giants of ancient Greece, Athens and Sparta, went to war against each other. Some city-states allied with Athens; others allied with Sparta. With its formidable army, Sparta was stronger as a land power. Athens had an excellent navy and was stronger as a sea power.

Twenty-seven years later, Athens and its allies lost the war. But Team Athens wasn't the only loser. The long war had weakened all the city-states. Vulnerable to attack, they were invaded and conquered by the Macedonians in 338 BCE, under Philip II.

When Philip II died in 336 BCE, his son Alexander the Great took over rule of Greece and the rest of the Macedonian kingdom. Two centuries later, Rome conquered Macedonia, including Greece. Ancient Greece gradually faded from its former glory—all except Athens, which continued to be an important cultural center.

Alexander the Great

Alexander was one of the greatest conquerors in world history. During his short life—he died when he was only thirty-three—he managed to conquer a vast empire that extended from Macedonia to Egypt and from Greece to India.

How Do We Know All This?

Historians and archaeologists rely on documents and artifacts left by the ancient Greeks. But we don't have all the pieces of the puzzle since it was a very long time ago. Furthermore, historians and archaeologists have different theories and interpretations regarding what, when, where, and so forth.

Still, we are lucky to have many remnants of the ancient Greek culture such as manuscripts, statues, pottery, jewelry, coins, musical instruments, tools, weapons, and temples and other buildings.

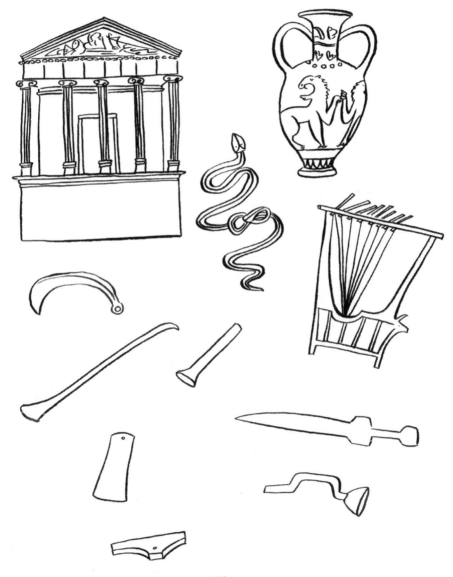

A Greek named Herodotus, who lived in the fifth century BCE, is often called the "father of history." He left behind a detailed account of ancient Greece as well as an account of the wars between the Greeks and the Persians.

An important part of the ancient Greek puzzle was solved in 1952, when an English architect named Michael Ventris deciphered some writing on very old clay tablets. The writing was a symbol-based language, and the translations provided a lot of information about how the earliest Greeks lived.

The Legacy of Ancient Greece

Ancient Greece truly was the cradle of Western civilization. You've already read about how they invented or contributed to a whole range of things: politics, philosophy, art, architecture, music, literature, math, science, medicine, and more—including the Olympics!

In addition, the ancient Greeks are credited with some cool inventions like the Archimedes screw (thanks to the mathematician Archimedes), which pumps water and is still used to irrigate crops. Another mathematician, Pythagoras, came up with the Pythagorean theorem, which is an important concept that has to do with the angles and sides of a triangle.

$$a^2 + b^2 = c^2$$

Well, it's been a great adventure. Good-bye, Ancient Greece!

Where to next?

Coming in July 2016!

Selected Bibliography

Ancient Greece by Anne Pearson, Alfred A. Knopf, 1992

The Ancient Greek World by Jennifer T. Roberts and Tracy Barrett, Oxford University Press, 2004

The Ancient Greeks by Charles Freeman, Oxford University Press, 1996

The Cambridge Illustrated History of Ancient Greece, edited by Paul Cartledge, Cambridge University Press, 1998

Encyclopedia Britannica Online, www.britannica.com

Encyclopedia Britannica Kids Online, www.kids.britannica.com

The Metropolitan Museum of Art (online), www.metmuseum.org

NANCY OHLIN is the author of the YA novels *Always, Forever* and *Beauty* as well as the early chapter book series Greetings from Somewhere under the pseudonym Harper Paris. She lives in Ithaca, New York, with her husband, their two kids, two cats, a bunny, and assorted animals who happen to show up at their door. Visit her online at nancyohlin.com.

ADAM LARKUM is a freelance illustrator based in the United Kingdom. In his fifteen years of illustrating, he's worked on over forty books. In addition to his illustration work, he also dabbles in animation and develops characters for television.